DEVIL IN THE WIND

voices from the
2009 black saturday bushfires

FRANK PREM

Published by Wild Arancini Press 2019

Copyright © 2019 Frank Prem

All rights reserved. No part of this publication may be reproduced, stored in a retrieval system, or transmitted in any form or by any means, electronic, mechanical, photocopying, recording or otherwise, without prior written permission from the publisher.

A catalogue record for this book is available from the National Library of Australia.

Disclaimer: This is a work of creative non-fiction, based on real life events as the author encountered them, through direct experience or observation, or in response to media reportage. Some names, places and identifying details may have been changed to protect privacy and maintain anonymity, and some identifying characteristics and details such as physical properties, occupations and places of residence may have been changed.

There has been no intent to include in this book any cultural or Indigenous references and language, but should any exist, they are included solely for the purpose of telling the story and are not meant to offend, or have any ill intent towards indigenous culture or people.

Every effort has been made to ensure that this book is free from overt error or omissions. However, the author, publisher, editor or their agents or representatives shall not accept responsibility for any loss or inconvenience caused to a person or organisation relying on this information.

Book cover design and formatting services by Self-Publishing Lab

First edition 2019

ISBN 978-0-9751442-6-8 (pbk)
ISBN 978-0-9751442-7-5 (e-bk)

For all those affected by wildfire.

*May our love for the bush remain,
while our hearts grow ever more resilient.*

Contents

Prologue 1

Devil in the Wind 13
   callignee butterflies 15
   evidence to the commission of enquiry: overview 17
   fire plan lament 20
   evidence to the commission of enquiry: the warning.........24
   chardy at the cellar door... 26
   evidence to the commission of enquiry: next time............27
   the hearth of home... 29
   evidence to the commission of enquiry: all in the ark for awhile 31
   a stubborn piece of mind... 33
   might have been 35
   evidence to the commission of enquiry: running like tar.. 36
   twisty twirling 37
   evidence to the commission of enquiry: communication difficulties... 38
   new heat 40
   evidence to the commission of enquiry: left flowerdale 41
   fathoming 44
   evidence to the commission of enquiry: like a duck on the lake 45
   update #1.. 48
   through the gauntlet... 49
   of strangers 51
   portraits in green and gold 52
   reserve one to marysville 55
   update #2...57
   what I miss.. 60
   the look of salvation 61

next	63
near and far	64
hope the sky	66
first bus to marysville	68
the strength of a truckie	70
ever again	72
the face is gone	74
obsession at the start	75
snorkel north	78
moving on	80
rebuilding for ferals	82
kinglake still	84
old man roo returns	85

Epilogue 87
   don decides 89
   reflections on the never ending 91

About the Author 94

Other Works by Frank Prem 95

What readers have said about
Small Town Kid by Frank Prem 96

Prologue

Devil In The Wind

oh my darling
the devil is in the wind
crying
roaring
swallowing sound
with every tongue
that licks to taste
the grass and trees

well
we could really only watch

it came down the hill
on both sides
and from behind us

four ways at once

Frank Prem

it speaks
to you

it speaks to you
in tongues
my darling

*the embers
were like an uzi
firing through every crack*

*doors
windows
skylights in the ceiling*

*if you were putting them out
at the top of the door
they swarmed in at the bottom*

it was like a live thing

Devil In The Wind

darling
my darling
there is sorrow on this ground

the devil's kiss
is a thirst
that cannot be quenched

look
I'm telling you my truck didn't burn
it melted

it just
bloody well melted

and the taste in your mouth
is the ash
and foul
of a love affair
to the death

I couldn't breathe

I just couldn't breathe

*we both had damp cloths
over our mouths
but I just
couldn't breathe*

*even now
I'm coughing up black*

Devil In The Wind

oh my darling
the world is different

so very different now
from when it first began

if we stayed in the house
another thirty seconds
we were dead

if we got in the car to drive away
we were dead
we could only back the sedan
onto blackened ground
sit in it
and watch our home burn down

it took just a few seconds

Frank Prem

darling
this
is the devil's
stamping ground

my animals
I need to go back in to save my animals

are you going to stop me
from going to them
they need me

are you trying to make me lose EVERYTHING

LET ME GO THROUGH

Devil In The Wind

this
is where he sings
of desecration

it's turned into a moonscape
in the space of three hours

it's going to take
oh
probably a couple of generations
for it to grow back

his sickling ground
to corrupt
with gouts of loathing

somebody lit it
on purpose

what do you do with someone like that

what on earth
do you do

Devil In The Wind

come away with me
my darling
come away

there is fire
in the red sun's eye

I'm not sure if this place
our home
for over twenty-five years
can ever feel the same for us

Frank Prem

there is nothing left
where the devil-wind
has blown

*my heart breaks
to say it*

*but I think
we've had enough
of living
in the wonderful
australian bush*

Devil in the Wind

callignee butterflies

butterflies have always lived
in our meadow

you can see them moving
everywhere you turn
in little flits
out of the corner of your eye

on this land we cleared
to make our home
they're as much a part
of every small thing
as we are

on black saturday
we might have gone
or might have stayed

there was nothing
to give us advice
better than our eyes
fixed on the thick smoke
at the back of the hill

when the air turned still
around us
it could have meant anything

in that eerie silence
who would know

Frank Prem

but ten tiny wraiths
fluttered to the floor
of our lounge room
looking for safety
as low down as they could get

and when the emptiness
started to roar we knew
we'd better run

it was time to go

evidence to the commission of enquiry: overview

1

well
the people up in the hills
where we live
were all chasing an uncomplicated ideal

for instance
my wife and I never watched tv
or opened up the daily paper

you see
all of us wanted to get away from that
and the whole town was full of people
who were much the same

yes it was hot that day
and yes
the blistering wind came from the north
but we're used to that
so the first I knew anything
of firestorms
was a blossom rising red
in the paddock stubble
of the block next door

I went out
to hurry up the neighbours
told them
now was time for them to go

and I waited at the bottom of the hill
for my wife and my son
until the leaf litter beneath my feet
began to glow

then I had to turn away

2

we didn't hear any warnings
over the radio
or anything like that
but
it was raining gum leaves
from out of the trees
for days and nights beforehand
so we knew something was up

3

I said to my wife

that fire's out of control

4

the guys in charge of the firefighters
thought marysville was still okay
but the place had already become ash and corpses
the night before

5

from the operations room
it was hard to keep track
and to know where was most needy
who to focus on

Devil In The Wind

there were hundreds of fires on the go
by that stage

6

the sound I heard
was like ten or twelve jumbo jets
down at the airport
all screaming their guts out
at the same time

7

well
before lunchtime on that day
I'd have said the fire-response system
in this state
was second to none
in the entire world

yes
that's what I would have told you
then

fire plan lament

I've heard
that my lifetime
has been an era of change

almost nothing
is the same
now
as it was when I was born

cars and planes
takeaway food
a computer and a phone
in every pocket

I couldn't have imagined
when I was small
that living an alternate life
online
could replace the summer days
that I spent walking in the bush
with my dog

but I suppose
you only really notice such things
when you look behind

we used to put the fires out
by hand
with wetted hessian bags
and knapsacks

Devil In The Wind

and somehow
we always seemed
to beat them down
or douse them

bulldozers
would carve a nine-foot break
to make the fires stop
and it was rare for a blaze
to ever leap the line

greenies weren't impressed
of course
said they made an ugly gash
in the forest

too wide
and to the detriment of nature

nowadays you can't go in
without proper training
too many *fire-ies* have been crisped
beside their machines

occupational health and safety
means most of the time
you just have to stand back
and let the red bastard run

a firebreak today
means trying to surround it
pushing the whole forest in
for acres all around
so eventually it'll eat itself out
cannibalised and starved

but it does no good
not really
because the bush is drier now
and these fires burn so hot

the wind
will nurture a shower of sparks
for miles at a time
and it doesn't rain any more
when you need it to

once upon a time you knew
that a change in the weather
would come
carrying good rain
the god-given rain
to cool it all down

but today I'm listening to sky cranes
dumping water
just the other side
of a brown billowing plume

and they're saying it again
on the radio
get your fire plans ready

shit
all they really mean is
make up your minds
will you stay or will you go

Devil In The Wind

and god bless you if you stay
when you've seen what happened
to those other poor tryers last week
didn't matter what they chose
they died just as dead whether at home
or out on the road

I'm tired of it
I wasn't born to meet change
the way it's happening now

I don't learn very well
under the pressure of my arse
being half incinerated

if this is how it has to be
then there's nothing *new*
that I really know

but I learnt at the breast
that you stay with it
right through to the very end

so this is my fire plan:
stand and fight
take the worst that comes

if I'm still upright when it's over
I'll shout the beer

if not
I'll see you on the other side
and it'll be your turn
to buy

Frank Prem

evidence to the commission of enquiry: the warning

I work as a spotter in the towers
over the summer months

my place is up on the ridge
about three kilometres out of marysville

from there on a clear day
I can see away off
to the horizon

when the first plume rises
it's my job to note coordinates
then get onto the airwaves
so the brigades can get there
to put it down

on that saturday I saw the first smoke
over by murrindindi mill
then it was over the top
around the black range
travelling west

I was on the line
as fast as I could make the call
because I could see
this thing would be big

but the radio did nothing
and the mobile phone wasn't answered
by the third failed attempt I knew
some people were going to die

Devil In The Wind

marysville is down in a hollow
and I didn't think it stood a chance
the smoke hit a thousand feet
and all the reply I got was
busy

I rang a friend
and told her to get out
because the fire bearing down
was a beastly size

I watched a spotfire light up
fourteen kilometres ahead of the front
while I was on the phone

I saw it began to run
and then
I felt terrified

the clouds went up another thousand feet
and ash and embers started falling
in a sort of hot black rain

the thing was alive
and I just shouted
good luck
down the phone
then
I bolted

they're saying that marysville
had no warning
but it's as true as I'm standing here
it wasn't because I didn't try

Frank Prem

chardy at the cellar door

henry and ev
put a shipping container underground
to make a wine cellar

when the smoke turned into flame
there was nowhere else to go

henry's still shaking his head
about the door
glowing red
while they watched

held prisoner
by the heat and the smell

he said

*what else could we do
we were feeling
quite shell-shocked
and knew we might die*

*as the hours passed we drank
five bottles*

*screw-top chardonnay I think it was
and a little too warm at that*

*but I couldn't crack the grange
without a bottle opener*

Devil In The Wind

evidence to the commission of enquiry: next time

we prepared meticulously for months
ahead of the hot season
cleared away any fuel and cut the grass

made sure there were no trees
too close to the house

we were ready

when the fire rating came across
on the warning system
I knew it was going to be bad
but I figured the numbers had to be wrong
because going years back to ash wednesday
which was a shocking set of fires
the rating only reached into the sixties
and on this day
it was hitting a hundred and sixty-five

still
we were ready
but my wife was so worried about it
that she rang everyone around us
all the young families
to tell them they should go

I think a few lives were saved
because of what she did

we first saw a bit of smoke
off in the distance
and then black embers started to drop

my wife went to put out a spotfire
but the soles on her shoes melted
when she jumped on the flames

we retreated to the house
and then the power failed

I shot out to the shed
to start the pump
but the petrol was all gone

evaporated

the wind changed and I got burned

as we ran
the house went up
just behind us

yes
we thought we were pretty right
to fight the fire that day
but every time I look
at the bandages on my arms
and the distorted face I see in the mirror
I tell myself
we need to do it better
next time

the hearth of home

everything happened so fast

I heard a roar
that sounded like jet planes

it came up the valley before me
and it came up the valley
behind

the rain was red
and the hail that hit my roof
was a barrage
of hot embers

I was showered by fire
fallen from the sky

I dropped the hose
and pulled a jacket flap up
over my face

then the windows exploded
flames flew in
sparks danced and I thought
I might be a goner
this time

but I pushed my panic away

chimneys are strong
and chimneys are tall

Frank Prem

chimneys seem to remain
when nothing else is left
so I crawled on my knees
through the black day and the sear

huddled in the hearth
where the fire usually lays
and I wept for my breath
while the beast burned my home
right to the ground around me

evidence to the commission of enquiry: all in the ark for awhile

well
you have to go back
to the chaos of that time

back to february

as the day got on
we realised we were in strife
because the thing was bigger and hotter
and faster and more unpredictable

it was more everything really

and we'd started to get word of huge losses
in other places around and about
people
property
animals
whole towns

so we were head-down-and-bum-up
and worried
about what was going to happen next

anyway
out of the smoke came a sort of convoy
led by a horse whose halter was held
by a woman driving a ute

in the back of the ute
a dog was running around
like a mad thing

after that came another car
with a float and two more horses

next was a vehicle that a police fellow
was driving

he'd been up in a chopper
trying to winch people out
but the wind got too big
so he dropped down and helped
by driving the car
with whoever he could get into it

then there were a couple of deer
that jumped out of the bush
when the cavalcade went past a clearing

and a pair of koalas

and three kangaroos

and some lizards

all running as part of the convoy

they scattered pretty quick
when the procession of them
emerged from the smoke
and the flames
but it was all in together
for a while

a stubborn piece of mind

she's crying
get out
down the phone

don't wait until the smoke
is already in the house

she's been watching the news
for days
looking at cars
that piled into each other
and burned
because the drivers couldn't see
through the dark
and the smoke

she's been taking note
of the way towns went up
all the places people tried to make
last stands

she's been learning
how a bushfire plan
that used to be as simple as either
go
or
stay and fight
was turned into a lie
because the nature of the beast
had changed

*don't you dare
sit on your backside waiting
don't dare
hope it'll turn out
for the best*

*get in your car and drive
now
while the road's still clear*

and she's wondering
what else can she do
an old man can be
such a stubborn fool

when she rings again
in the morning
he just better be alive
so she can give him
every little bit
of a damn good piece
of her mind

might have been

I was away at work
in wodonga
as the temperature rose

my wife
phoned when the power
and the air-conditioner went off

she could see the glow
from over murmungee way
through the back window

later
listening to the radio together
we heard
of the houses gone
and the lives of two people lost
in mudgegonga

strangers to us
and yet
so close

Frank Prem

evidence to the commission of enquiry: running like tar

when I saw her emerge
from out of the smoke
it was just ...

I didn't know what to do

she was obviously distressed
in real trouble

and her feet
were sort of ...

see
she had no shoes
or anything at all over them
and I don't know
how far she must have come
but they were ...

it looked as though
they were dripping ash

like tar
pouring off her feet

she was a terrible mess
and I had no idea
what on earth
I should do

twisty twirling

well
as you know
I've been fighting fires
for over thirty-five years now

but I've never seen them
behave like that before

see
we're in the middle of a big paddock
and out of nothing
comes a shimmering pillar
of flame

twirling around itself
like a fiery tornado

it skipped across the paddock
hardly bothering to touch down

except that wherever it went
sort of erupted in red
and fire started running
in every direction
out from the centre

was mesmerising
and it would have been a marvel
just to sit back and watch
if the twisty hot bastard
wasn't dancing its way
right up behind us

Frank Prem

evidence to the commission of enquiry: communication difficulties

our fire station didn't have the internet
and the captain had to race back home
to get his laptop

it ran wireless
so we could use that
to keep checking out the website
for updates
and for the warnings

when we were out
in the fire
we had a moment
when the mobile phone actually worked
and we tried to call in an ambulance
but nobody came

so we picked up this body
that was mostly cooked flesh
and blisters
and pain

put him on one of our ladders
and I drove the truck
as slow as I could
but
with trees falling down around us
in a dance of sparks
and mustard-yellow smoke
that I could hardly see through
it was a rough enough ride
I guess

Devil In The Wind

the ambulance finally arrived
after we got back to the station
but they were too late
or I'd taken too long
or he never had much chance anyway
with so much of his body burned

but there are times
even with a poor hopeless case like he was
when I wake
in the middle of the night
with the smell of him in my nose

times when I wish
there was someone I could talk to
who might understand

new heat

a river of aluminium flowed out
from beneath the hulk of our car

engine blocks are only alloy
these days

window frames on houses
swam away
and cement sheeting
turned to powder

heat

it's an old word

we need something new
to describe what ran through us
that day

Devil In The Wind

evidence to the commission of enquiry: left flowerdale

well
I was going to stay and fight
it's always been my plan
that if a fire came
I'd be ready

I installed sprinklers on the roof
had a ten-thousand-litre water tank
with a pump primed
and right to go

I thought about what I would do
and all in all I have to say
I was satisfied

but I changed my mind that afternoon
when I saw what the fire was doing
to the trees

you see I noticed they were twisting around
just about being unscrewed
right out of the paddock

I drove away with my lights on full
and my hand stuck down on the horn
as a way of warning

I was petrified

~

in flowerdale
we gathered around the pub
and kept an eye on the school

there were spotfires here
and small blazes there
right though the afternoon

at some point they brought in an old man
who'd been burned

they carried him in on a plastic chair
and we laid him down on the floor
used wet towels
to try to take the heat away

while a few did that
the rest fought on
and somehow we battled right through
that dark red night

~

in the morning
it was a chainsaw job
to get back up the road
to my home

it was burned down of course
there was bugger all
that survived the blaze

walking down the road in front of my land
I saw two bodies beside a burnt-out car
I've since found out they were a mother
and her son

Devil In The Wind

another car had crashed into a tree
with one more soul lost
and in that moment
it looked to me as if
god
had just abandoned flowerdale

fathoming

it's hard to fathom

every place on the road went up
except ours

the kids
asked me
if we were going to die

they were crying
when we made a run for it
through alien country
that I thought I knew
like the back of my hand

and up there
do you see that wretched
scrubby-looking shack

mad mick lived there
poor bastard

he topped himself
a few weeks ago
and nobody's gone near the place since
but it's still standing
in one piece

I can't work any of it out

evidence to the commission of enquiry: like a duck on the lake

I was lying in the mud
of the lake that's in the middle
of marysville
staring up
at a flock of ducks
that might have saved my life

up above my head
the fire was leaping through the trees
around me

orange fingers were dancing forward
hungry for something more
to burn

it looked alive
like a modern-day cartoon
it was hyper-real
and yet
I couldn't believe it was true

I found my hand was reaching
searching
for a remote control

I think I meant
to make it small
or turn it off

drive it further away

Frank Prem

I'm from the third generation of my family
to live in our little hill town
and I made my living
by playing music
for tourists
and the passing trade

but I saw the guesthouse burn down
and smelled the death
of the old piano
that was sort of like
a familiar
to me

the ducks
have always made me laugh
and brought a real pleasure
over the years

I've watched them gather
on so many nights
all around the reed beds
there
in the water

and I thought
if it was good enough for them
it might do just as well
for a man in trouble
like me

so when the smoke was sitting
just above my head
frothing and bubbling
with all the nasty promise
of a cauldron filled with tar

Devil In The Wind

and the sky caught fire
while embers fell
like rain in a meteor shower
white with heat

I walked into the lake
up to my neck

and I prayed to god
to save me

update #1

it's still burning but ...

so far ...

three towns
are no longer on the map

over a hundred
are said to have died

eighteen hundred homes are ash
on the ground

three and a half thousand are up in the hills
still fighting fires

seven thousand are hoisting new villages
of tents

and one is being held
in custody

through the gauntlet

in a little town
outside warburton
there's nothing left in main street

everyone's gone
and the shops are closed
for the duration

one man
alone
and sweeping the path
in front of a cafe
says

I reckon it's all been overhyped
if we didn't fry
last week when it was really hot
today should be a doddle

but the procession
along the highway out of town
is taking no chances

and the sign
at the corner of the pub
where the menu is usually posted
has summed it up
for almost everyone
and everything

where it used to read
rump steak special
thirteen dollars ninety-five

now
there's advice
on offer for free

RUN!

of strangers

a lot of our backyards
are wearing the brown signs
of singeing
but the town is still standing
and every one of us is alive
thanks to strangers

who've come from one hundred
two hundred
they've come from three hundred miles away
to look after us

we're dazed and disoriented
with heatstroke and fire blight
smoke haze and embers
bush burning and tear streaks

yet
we're alive
thanks to the good strong hearts
of strangers

Frank Prem

portraits in green and gold

when I was a teenager
I helped to do what they called
mopping up

a knapsack on my back
clambering all over
what seemed like mountains
but were in reality
just modest hills

hard work
for a young sapling such as I was

at the end of a shift
we were fed triangle sandwiches
made by the ladies auxiliary
and just wanted to have a bath
or to sleep

these days
when I see a man in yellow
lying on the ground
exhausted
I know what he's been doing
with great certainty

~

Devil In The Wind

he looks straight ahead
but I don't think he can see anything
his eyes are too much of water
and a little out of sync
while the dirty soot and scorch
stained on his face and hands
tell most of the story

he's been wearing yellow
and a helmet
for about nine days
stumbled now to a two-hour break
because you have to stop sometimes
try to chew through a sandwich
and take a drink that isn't flavoured
by eucalyptus burning

stretched out on the ground
the grass is enough for a pillow

he doesn't notice
doesn't care
and right away he's sleeping

for he has aimed the hose
and grappled with the urgency of water
under pressure
run for his life
from flames the wind had leaping
returned again to hold the line
to let evacuees make good
run again
returned

you cannot countermand an act of god
you can only buy some time
and he has spent himself hard
given almost all he has
in a pool of sweat and tears
each aimed at a hot lick of flame

the effort may have blackened
some part of his soul
and he can't quite remember
what it's like
to feel entirely human

but two hours have already passed
the horn is blaring
another firefighting implement is ready
to take position
at one more place of heat and flame
and driving wind

so he gathers together his pieces
takes a rattled breath and cough
to clear the throat
then stands and staggers
to the truck

it's time to be moving

reserve one to marysville

on tv
they're in camouflage
floppy hats and war paint
there's always one studying a map
then pointing forward
before the troop becomes visible
out of cleverly disguised places of concealment
that the camera never saw

join the reserve
learn combat skills and leadership

in the reserve we'll show you
how to land a chopper
in the dark

the way to fire a gun

over

out

modern radio
we know how to talk to you

join the reserve

~

alright listen up
don't forget
this has been a battle zone
and we're here
straight after

*it's been a shooting war
that's left its char-marks
everywhere
in the rubble*

*so work forward slowly
house to house
and shed to shed
from fallen wall
to sheet of tin*

*and be cautious
with any suspicious mound*

*take your time
engage all your senses
and be wary
what you disturb*

*get the dogs
if you're not sure
they're experts at this*

*but
if you're the one
to find the reason we're here
have a care*

*don't touch anything
just call it in*

*that's our job
today*

update #2

the fires started
fourteen days ago

delburn and the bunyip park
went even earlier

then
it was kilmore east
wandong
and horsham

murrundindi mill and marysville
eaglehawk and redesdale

beechworth

wilsons promontory
the dandenongs
and the yarra valley

from daylesford to the otways
and even french island

three big fires remain
burning

one million acres of forest
have been converted
into an uncounted number
of blackened sticks

god alone knows
how to measure the life
in a million acres

five hill towns
have now become empty streets
lined by ashen allotments
that can only be identified
by their map references

over a hundred and seventy are said
to have died
the toll is still being counted

they fell in twenty-four different places
that lost eighteen hundred and thirty-four
good homes

the effort to respond
numbered more than ten thousand
who came to help
from all over australia
and from around the world

the seven and a half thousand
who were shepherded or fled somehow
are settling into tents
and too soon they'll greet
the frosty nights
of autumn

three started fires that killed
in fourteen different places

they're being held and charged
and all that gruesome rigmarole

Devil In The Wind

the weather
is so nice today
but
the bureau is concerned that
next friday
might be a rerun
of the extremes just gone

what will we name that day
if the devil calls
to dance with us
again

what I miss

kookaburras and magpies
wattlebirds
fantails

the black cockatoos
and gang gangs

so many honeyeaters
they were a wonder

we had them all

I counted over fifty
species
that visited our property

only a small two acres
but
fifty species

imagine

spinebills and thornbills

robins
and the grey thrush

more than anything
I miss
the birds

the look of salvation

for countless days
there's been nothing to talk about
but fires

it feels as though
it could have been a year
already

wave after wave of catastrophe *show*
and disaster *tell*
wherever we turn

we've hardly come to terms
with what's happened
but the warnings
are already being issued
for next week

and next month
and another year that will be too hot
to live

the cathedral in town
threw open its doors yesterday
high church
staid faith and tried tradition
came together to hymn their prayers

I could hear the congregation rustling
in the aisles

tinder dry

and calling on the same old heaven
to explain the way the devil works

asking us to accept
and forgive

that's how it's always been

but in the pub
they're telling stories
about survival
and of those who've passed away

there's still soot
etched into the creases
on their hands
while they take a blow
between firestorms

they talk about who needs help
and who might yet want saving

I look across the top
of a low-church glass of beer
for the answer to a prayer

next

now it's musk
and ballan

lyonville
newbury
and sailors falls

wombat's been mentioned
wheatsheaf
and spargo creek

I wonder if
lerderderg and bullengarook
will still be there
tomorrow morning

near and far

yesterday in daylesford
you
were listening to public radio
while the fires were threatening
around our doors

tuning in to urgent alerts
repeated each half hour

you could almost taste our smoke
rising behind the buckland gap
up by dederang
and over near yackandandah

eventually you'd heard enough
had to get on the phone to call
just to hear our voices reassure

we're okay

today in beechworth
we
are listening hard
to our own radio

there's an urgent alert
for musk vale
and bullarto

and we're starting
to go crazy
thinking about your fire

hearing everything
that's being said

Devil In The Wind

over the airwaves
and knowing nothing at all

hello
hello
is that you
are you okay

tell us
what's going on

we've been
so worried

hope the sky

we were warned it could be
catastrophe
all over again

that
too much wind
would fan the flames

schools were closed
the children told to stay home
under parental watch

~

last night at two a.m.
I tuned in
to the national broadcaster

instead of sport
from johannesburg
there was a live cross
to the weather bureau

the change had bypassed
some little town
and was on its way
to a different place
further east

but there were
no new fires
to announce

~

Devil In The Wind

before I woke this morning
I dreamed the bells were pealing out
from the cathedral
up on church street hill

and when I opened eyes
the sound I heard
was tiny rain
pattering on the roof

falling drops
creating damp spots
on the path
and I prayed the sky
was full to overflowing

first bus to marysville

it's been a slow ride

but
we're coming into town at last

that's where julia lived
poor girl
with her kiddies
and ken
the sheep and a dog

look around

there's no life
beneath the forest of charcoal sticks
that was once a kind of meaning for us

that we were so proud of

the grey powder lying there
was grass
and the stuff of our gardens

we might as well be on the moon

I can't see my home
through the army boys and girls

can't picture that we used to live
where forensics are sifting ash
and melted iron

and it's impossible
to think

Devil In The Wind

above the sounds
that have filled this bus
with keening
but I hear well enough
the crying of the breeze
rattling bare branches

I'm shivering

take me back down the hill
to the tents
I can't bear to look
anymore

take me out of this grave
that used to be marysville

take me away
I've seen it all

Frank Prem

the strength of a truckie

yes
and I'm just a truckie
from up canberra way

I gave up my time
because I could

took a load of square bails south
where they'll be handfeeding their beasts
for weeks into months
until the rain comes

there'll be no green pick
for a cow or a sheep
down there

the cockies around canberra
burned out in two thousand and three
and there's not too much going spare
this year
but they remember the help that came
while they were all still black
and bewildered

so I loaded my rig
and headed for the border
another eleven blokes came behind me
on the freeway

Devil In The Wind

now I'm a bloody big guy
and I can be a hard man
you have to be strong
to survive
in a tough old game

but I couldn't believe
what I saw
when I topped the last of the hills

and I feel no shame
in telling you
I had to stop my rig
by the roadside
and cover my eyes

ever again

off in the corner
of the new temporary classroom
is where we put
the donated-clothes hamper

unobtrusive
because we don't want to make
a big thing of it

if the kids need anything
they can just go off and get it

this is the new normal
for a while

and all of them have lost
something

maybe everything

they're doing the best they can
the kids

good days
bad days

this morning though
was a bit left field

a young fella went up
to the hamper

crawled right inside it

buried himself in the clothes
and wouldn't come out

took two and a half hours
to get him to speak

it turned out
he was petrified
that nothing was going to stand still
or stay the same
long enough to trust

ever again

the face is gone

he's alive
but he's lost his garden

perhaps he's lost
his soul

he carved men from trees
nymphs asleep
beneath shady branches

a bracken bower
as a home
for creatures that amaze

so
what's a man to do

when the meaning of his life
the place where he smoothed
the face of god
is gone

what
is a man to do[1]

---

[1] Bruno's art and carvings can be visited online at: www.brunosart.com.

obsession at the start

it's beautiful up in the hills
now

hard to believe
two months have already gone by

it seems such a long time

yet
just like yesterday

and the places where the fire burned
are clear to see

not black so much
as brown

and grey

rust-deadened swathes
where the flames pressed their lips
to kiss farewell

coming home the long way
from mount beauty
down into bright
through myrtleford
then up again at the gapsted turnoff
towards home

a farmer
at the fence-line by the road
is stringing wire through new posts

burnt places snuggle both sides
of the bitumen
dead branches overhead

rust and death
and grey

here
just out of town
at library road
is where our blaze started
you can see the very place
where the powerline fell

amazing how it spread
not close to us
not far enough away

~

and from gippsland
there's news

the police are
knowingly
making empty statements

they found the place
they know the time
they've tracked every man and woman
every child

narrowed down

Devil In The Wind

they say that he was thereabouts
they say he told a lie
they say he makes no easy friendships
that he likes fire
a member
of the local volunteer brigade

shhhh

they can't say a name
because he wouldn't be safe in town
from the locals
who are his neighbours

mister firestarter
lit one
became three
ate the town
and left just discoloured white ash
in small mounds

mister firelighter wore yellow
manned a hose
he is obsessed with fighting blazes
and saving lives

snorkel north

it's a bit ironic
really

while you poor southerners
away down in victoria
are being burnt for weeks on end
we've got the opposite problem

funny old country this one
we spend about ten months of the year
praying for rain
but right now we're cursing it

it was just after new year
that the wet began
and when it came
it poured

we'd get a foot of rain
in a night
and then we had to line up
for more

our roads have been cut off
for about eight weeks now
and it'll be another couple of months
before we can get a car
onto some of the tracks
let alone a truck to shift the cattle out
and make a quid again

the food drops are great
but sometimes we feel like
we've been forgotten

Devil In The Wind

in amongst the bigger disasters
down your way

normanton will be buggered
after this
and all of us up here
in debt for years
or busted and gone
before we know it

I feel really sorry
for you poor folk
it's got to be pretty horrible
and some of you
must be doing it tough
but
spare a thought
if you get a lazy second

don't forget normanton
and all of us
swimming around in circles
up north

moving on

there is a kind of irony
that becomes evident
in the post-apocalyptic optimism
of some survivors

a tendency to downplay
severity

there is acknowledgement of the efforts
that went into saving lives
and property
but
with qualifiers

... the volunteers were brilliant
you know
worked their arses off for us
but
some funny things happened ...

recognition of the cost
that comes with being saved

... the B & Bs
were choc-a-block full
with fire-fighters
but they didn't
well they couldn't
really
charge them

so they sort of
donated ...

Devil In The Wind

and ultimately
a ready acceptance
that life
has to go on
and quickly at that

... gotta run
I've got a barbie tonight ...

rebuilding for ferals

see
flowerdale was sort of purposefully
built out on the fringes
and up in the bush

it had a particular ...

... character

like
I mean people revelled in the fact
we had no police station

no one breathing down anyone's neck
about regulation right
and regulation wrong
and all that

there's a few of them
up in the hills
had good reason
to keep well out of sight
if you get my drift

it sort of tells you something
when you think how
the whole bunch of us got together
and battled our hearts out
to save the most important building
in the town

Devil In The Wind

the pub

it was important before all this
absolutely vital now
and nearly the only place left standing
because of what we did

anyway
there's no question about it
flowerdale just has to be rebuilt

there's got to be room in this world
for a few ferals like us
as well

kinglake still

kinglake is dead
spread out on the ground

streets to nowhere
flanked by blank allotments

kinglake is in a twilight dream
holding on to itself

rows of tents
in temporary permanence
on football grounds
below the hills

kinglake is on life support
breathing slow

in small steps
between guy ropes
to the laundry and the showers

kinglake is rising
in the morning

going off to school with mum

full of plans to clear the block
of debris
and twisted memories

kinglake is alive
and taking shape

a picture being drawn again
in a sketchbook
of the heart

old man roo returns

the kangaroo is back

we call him *old man roo*
and I first bumped into him
in the backyard
a few years ago

didn't think of him at the time
but when I was crawling out
through the smoke and the flames
I assumed he was dead
like the rest of the wildlife
around here

then yesterday morning
he was there again
beside the water tank

so I scrounged around
asked the neighbours
if they had anything left

got hold of a small bale
of lucerne hay

I'm feeding him now
a bit of it each day

there's no need for any of us
to do it tougher
than we have to

Epilogue

don decides

don across the road
is smiling tonight
putting his kids into the back seat
of the car

two little girls
they're babbling about the dog
about school today
about something

and he looks around
like he can't believe
it's all just the way
it's supposed to be

on that terrible saturday
he packed the sedan
doused the walls of the house
with water

covered the motorbike
and left it out on the roadside

settled the girls
then cast his eye over
the bare paddocks
that border mellish street
and across to the smoke
rising up
from the buckland gap

said a mental goodbye
took his darlings away
to safety

today
he's wondering
if he really should have gone

the fire didn't get this far
after all

but he looks at his girls

holds them close

and knows he'll do it again
exactly the same
anytime smoke rises

Devil In The Wind

reflections on the never ending

and I wonder
when will this thing end

each time I put down my pen
I think it's done
I've heard enough of these hard stories

there's only so much
that one person can take in
and I
am just like anybody else
I want bad things to fade away
to nothing
and then I might move on

but each day
there's news from the inquiry

somebody's story
takes my breath
and I am moved
by the poetry of pain and fear
and raw honesty
released in the cadence of their voices

I don't need to read the papers
to know that winter is here
there have been six days in a row of frost
and a blanket of snow
up around the black-scoured hills

where town remnants are shivering
in tents and caravans
and the charred remains

of incinerated hopes and dreams
haven't yet been cleared away

I wrote another story of survival
that I heard just yesterday
when I read it to my wife
she wept

I guess it hasn't ended yet

and perhaps it must go on

to ensure we remember

to ensure survivors
can still tell their tales

and to ensure
there is a place of safekeeping

a refuge
for these stories
forged in hell

About the Author

Frank Prem has been a storytelling poet for forty years. When not writing or reading his poetry to an audience, he fills his time by working as a psychiatric nurse.

He has been published in magazines, online zines and anthologies, in Australia and in a number of other countries, and has both performed and recorded his work as 'spoken word'.

He lives with his wife in the beautiful township of Beechworth in North East Victoria, Australia.

Frank's web page is located at www.FrankPrem.com

Other Works by Frank Prem

Small-Town Kid (2018)

What readers have said about Small Town Kid by Frank Prem:

Small Town Kid is a wonderful collection.
With so few words Frank Prem is able to paint a picture so vivid you can't help but get lost in the story. Whether he's talking about family, a picnic, a trip to the butcher or even the outside toilet it's difficult not to become immersed in the words and imagine yourself right there with him. Cover to cover this is an excellent read. –ST

~

From the dedication poem, "I Can Hardly Wait to Show You", to "Circular Square Town", Frank Prem's chronological journey from infancy to the present has a familiar feel to it. Almost as if you were taking a walk through your own memory lane to recall the innumerable small, but unforgettable moments that make up a life. Frank's style is minimalist, with plenty of room to fill in the blanks with your own conjecture or possible parallel memories. Written about an Australian town that was a gold-rush centre in its day, it touches on those times as well as describes the landscapes there. Frank's work is approachable, understandable, and sensitive in its handling of the most delicate of subjects. –JL

~

Small Town Kid is filled with rich memories of childhood and family. Frank's poems paint vivid pictures of a time when the rhythms of life were less hurried. This poetry collection comes together into a joyous, warm quilt of memories. –MMc

This book of poems is an intriguing and insightful look at country towns – one of my favourite subjects. The book has poems that show an Australia that's gone – or is it? The stories are wonderful, closely entwined with the people and place. It will bring a smile, maybe a wink, and you will enjoy every word. -CD

~

This could be any small town, and any child. If you could extract the peculiarly Australian nuances and replace them with others, the poems might be about a small town anywhere and any child who grew up in it. The poems are presented in an order showing the boy growing up from his earliest years through to reaching young adulthood, taking the reader on a journey alongside him. And they have the power to transport you there. (He) writes sparingly, knowing like an artist when to stop. But everything is there, and the writing invariably has beauty no matter what its subject matter. Unhesitatingly, I give this book five stars. -MC

~

I recognize a true storyteller when I see one, and Frank Prem definitely fits the description. Like the minstrels of old, he tells his stories in a lilting, musical format that conjures up pictures, even in non-poetry people like me. And isn't that exactly what minstrels are supposed to do? As a New Australian of Eastern European heritage, much of Frenki's life resonates with me, and yet, it's the imagery of time and place that makes these poems familiar to all Australians. And perhaps to non-Australians as well. Boy hood and the wonder years. Some things are universal. Highly recommended. -AF

www.ingramcontent.com/pod-product-compliance
Lightning Source LLC
Chambersburg PA
CBHW052028290426
44112CB00014B/2423